Final Sun

Patrick Nipp

Copyright © 2012 Patrick Nipp
All rights reserved.
ISBN-13: 978-1724538192
ISBN-10: 1724538195

DEDICATION

I dedicate this book to my beautiful mom and amazing dad who taught me that there are so many ways to fix a problem. I also want to dedicate this book to my brother Joey, and my Aunt Gabbie. I wanted to write a book that would appeal to many different types of people. I also want people to know there's not just "Yes" and "No" answers to everything With so many solutions out there, we can fix any problem.

Thanks so much for supporting me through everything.

ACKNOWLEDGEMENT

I would like to acknowledge my best friend, Chase who always read my poetry and encouraged me to seek publication.. I want to acknowledge my teacher Ms Laramie. I always loved her quote< "Fake it till you make it".

Hope of a Rose

The grass flows
With the music
The life of a rose
Winter it lies in ruin

Don't let it stay
Cause like the rose
You don't let it stay
Then you pose

Let the sunshine
Hit your leaves
With a lovely shine
And you believe

That it will get better
Give a friend a hug
Let it be neater
Like that lovely bug
On that leaf

Storming

The storm is dark and black
With flashes of lightning
They're on the attack
It's frightening

I wish the sun will come back
It will let sunlight in
So there is no more black

It's like a sin, it goes away

The world is bright
Full of beauty
Full of lovely light
The black is no beauty

The wind is powerful
Like the lightning crashing
 I wish I was powerful
So it will start fleeing

The rain is gone
The wind is gone
The lightning is gone
But life is not gone

Words Can Slay

They say sticks and stones can break
My bones but words will never hurt if
They knew what was said they would break
It makes me so stiff

Their words would choke and kill me
It feels like a sword impaling my chest
They do it for free
Just please give me a rest

I'm sorry I can't be perfect
Why do you have to slay me with a blade
No one cares you go unchecked
Why are you so keen in setting a blockade

Then when I got sick you gave me hell
Now I'm slitting my throat
And I'm letting out a yell
I'm dead now why don't you gloat

That you killed me with your words
So next time don't slay, pray
Everyday with the birds
And don't make someone your prey

Sin Cutting

You drive me insane
With your cutting
But you say you're sane
I'm afraid your gonna start gutting

Why do you do it
You paralyze me
I'm afraid your gonna slit
Your throat it really hurts me

That I can't stop you
I can barely stand
Every time it turns me blue
Just remove your hand

From my soul
And quit blaming it on me
It's taking its toll
I'm at sea

Drowning in my own thoughts
Just someone pull me out
What's your plots
Cause they're working and I'm blacking
   out

Uplifting Rats

I see people putting others down
I can't believe they could do that
How come it doesn't make you drown
That you keep calling them a rat

Grow up a little
Quit pretending
You put some of them in mental hospitals
Why don't you start defending

Raise people up
Make them confident
Stop making a mess and pickup
Be nice put them in astonishment

Who knows they might be really fun
And maybe you'll fall in love
Maybe they're loved one
If so you'll fly like a dove

Heartstrings

Why do you think I'm not going to make it
Do you not believe in me
Wait till I'm a big hit
Capitalise your gonna wish we were not apart a sea

Cause I'm being lifted
This is what God wants with me
That's why he made me gifted
He has me swimming in a talent sea

I know I can count on him
With him I'll never fall
He gave me a trim
So I don't have to brawl

To make it in life
I've got a great set of skills with
Words so sharp they cut like a knife
It's not a myth

Heartstrings (cont.)

Just read my other poems
Be careful it will pull your heartstrings
And I'll be one of the greatest poets
It'll wrap your heart with emotion strings

Every word you read it will pull harder
Into it has squeezed all your tears out
And it makes you as heavy as a anchor
So take this inspiration and sprout

Do what you believe in
Let no one stop you
And go out there in win
Make everyone talk about how you flew

Just keep your head up
And keep going
And even if you have to backup

Heart of Gold

They say I have a heart of gold
They say it's polished and shiny
 And it will never grow old
They say it's huge not tiny

They love that I care for others
And will die for anyone
As if they were all my brothers
Cause I know I've won

The race in life
With time to spare
They say I'll get a lovely wife
And we'll be a great pair

They say I will have an amazing son
That acts just like me but better
My son and I will have fun
Making people's life better

But my son being like his father
He would save someone too
He will run farther
Than me and have a great life too

Must Protect

What if I ended it all
Killed myself how would you feel
So I could fall
And let the devil steal

My precious soul
I feel like I deserve it
I'm stuck in a hole
With emotion spikes that split

My soul and my heart
I can't take this pain anymore
I wish I can have a new start
Because I have a tainted core

Then you came along it helped
We've been on a roller coaster
But sometimes I feel unhelped
Like a imposter

I might be losing my mind
I feel every chip and crack in my armor
But I learned I must be kind
And a charmer

But now My armor is gone
My life is gone
My soul is gone
But your not gone

Steel Linked Souls

Brother we have linked souls
It makes us strong enough
To cut jewels
Our souls are very tough

We're two of a kind
No one can be sweeter than us
We'll hit our steel to make you blind
So don't mess with us

I will die for him
I will take a beating for him
I will kill for him
But you won't hurt him

I know he will do the same
Because our bond is strong
You can't put out our flame
Just admit that you're wrong

Prairie of Death

When I write from the heart
It's dark and scary
But I thought I had a pure heart
I'm left alone on a prairie

Scared and lost with no way to go
I feel like I'm losing it
My mind is my only foe
My brain split

One side is calm
The other is wild
It wants to create a bomb
So I can be exiled

I wish someone could understand
Maybe I'm crying for attention
I can't even stand
I feel the tension

I'm trying to control myself
Its very hard
Maybe I'll kill myself
I can't because It's hard

Just someone save time
Kill me
I'm suffering so make it peacetime
And finish me

Clean Souls

We will fight and stare death in the face
Stand together nothing can destroy us
We're stronger than steel face it
We'll turn your negative to a plus

Together no one stands alone
If we do we break and fall apart
You're weak cause you stand alone
You can change though and play your part

Instead of destroying create
Instead of darkness shine light
We'll give you a clean slate
Then you'll see you don't have to fight

I know you feel empty inside
I know it hurts
Just stand by our side
Because we have pure spirits

Nature's Soul

The butterflies flutter about
And dances with the leaves
The sun is out
It glimmers on the leaves

The sun smiles down on the earth
We would die without it
So we love the sun and the earth
It's really lit

Mother nature keeps the water clean
And our soul pure
We trust and can lean on the earth that's so clean
Because mother nature kept the earth pure

Wanted Beauty

It's bad when your family doesn't Love you
It brings me tears every time
It's nothing new
It hurts every time

All I wanted was a happy birthday
But that's to much for y'all
It makes me so grey
That's why I'm sweet and kind to all

I don't want people to feel unwanted
I'll tell everyone they're beautiful
So they feel wanted
And now there joyful

It destroys me but it helps everyone
I will never be like you
I'll put a smile on for everyone
So no one turns out like you

Uplink

The music speaks to my soul
It goes with the rhythm of my heart
It's a very special jewel
Made of art

The melody helps me think
And keeps me from being stressed
It seems like it uplinks
The music helps me rest

The music is at best
With my family
They also feel it in there chest
It helps us bond our family

In all good time
The music must rest
So we tell it good night
Then we rest

Second Family

I wanted to write poetry
But I didn't think it would work
I feel like writing helps with anxiety
So I started to work

Then my friends found out
They pushed me further
Now I have no doubt
They are my observers

My friends are like my second family
I love them to death
Screw it they are my family
I would stare death down

I would take arrow after arrow
So they can live
They'll make a row
And takes hits for me cause they want me to live

I would die for y'all
So y'all can live one more day
I will crawl
So you can live another day

One more thing
I'm going to make it big time
Thanks for taking off my anchor ring
Now it's show time

My World

I'm going to tell
That I love you
I hope this isn't a spell
I Hope we stick like glue

So please tell me
I love you too
We can go for tea
Then the zoo

Love as high as a mountain
You're my world
I'll drink from your love fountain
To be your world
Too

Sailing Sun

What do you not understand
I make mistakes
I wish you would understand
Let's take a retake

Like a selfie
Till it's perfect
It only take three
Let's not neglect

So let's try again
Then we'll sail
With the wind to gain
Even if it hails

We'll keep pushing
All the way
So get you're footing
It's still day

So as the sun sets
If we stay the course
With regrets
Our destiny is set

Sailing Sun (cont.)

So let's shape our future
With no regret
Let's be the ruler
With no regret

We are the rulers
Of our destiny
No one else can rule
Cause we leave a legacy

Once I'm an ancestor
They'll be in awe
I'm not a jester
So they stand there in awe

I believe we'll make it
Do you believe
So get your wit
And believe

We are sailing again
With no hail
And an adventure to gain
So hoist that sail

Faith of Love

How Can I express
All this love
It's so much stress
Like a beach with no cove

I wish you would be mine
We can laugh together
And twine
Just sign with this feather

On this paper
At the bottom
Love as high as a skyscraper
We'll never hit bottom

Don't Change

I love your kindness
And your smile is so sweet,
so righteous
It's pretty neat

Please never change
You're loved by all
The sun is in range
Please don't uninstall

One day you'll find a man
That can treat you right
I know you can
I can see it in sight

Poison

Your like a poison sting
Small but deadly
And you're lingering
I'm barely
Here

I feel the walls falling
At the speed of light
And you keep calling
Isn't that a sight

I'm not answering
Cause I'll be in a spiral
Again I'm concealing
Like a person on trial

I'm moving on
You should too
like the wish upon
Your gone too

Smile

When Love falls like a dark
Night when the sun comes down
Smile and embark
Again, But let that frown

Stay no longer
Cause the sun will come
Let that smile conquer
Like a beating drum

No more chains
You are free to love
With the reins
Of true love

By your side
You're happy again
With a lovely bride
And a kid to gain

Final Sun

Listen Then Teach

You don't have to die
To start over
Quit being shy
Make some friends amd play red rover
Or go skip a rock
All you have to do is knock

Build a bond with them
Let that start your revival
You plus them equals a sum
You will be great at survival
Y'all will make a team
I promise it's not a dream

That feeling in your chest
Is happiness
Don't get stressed it's not a test
It's happiness
Just remember that's your revival
It's not survival

Just lean on each other
And teach others
This lesson
All you have to do is listen

All Mine

Sometimes I feel like breaking down
Cause everything is on my shoulders
But I decide not to frown
And yes it still smolders
Now I've got you in my life
One day I hope you can be my wife

We've been there for each other
Through thick and thin
And I know you'll make a great mother
I know I can win
Cause I've got you
You surprise me with something new

Someone that actually cares
And you always give me hugs
With me and you there are no tears
And neither of us slugs
Cause we got each other
And we always see farther

All I need is you
You're so beautiful
And I hope I can keep you
Cause your so wonderful
I love you so much
You always touch
My heart
It's just like art

Life Of A Student

Lets go skip rocks
Down by the shore
Then we can go to the dock
We can jump in and swim to the floor

We'll have all our friends there
And will laugh and have fun
With a cool breeze of air
The next day will realize we should've stayed
    out of the sun

We'll walk down the stage
With our heads high
They'll say we matured to our age Then we'll throw our hats to the sky

Walking out with our experience
Our defeats
Our attitude that's serious
We'll walk into the streets
With our high school experience

Show Up

Don't let people stop you
Just keep moving
Keep believing and stay true
Start improving

Show them you can
And show them you're the best
Just don't procrastinate, plan
Don't become stressed

Just know that you can do it
Stay strong
Just hit it
Headstrong

Final Sun

Thanks everyone for reading my book. I really appreciate everyone that pushed me to finish this book. Do me a favor. No matter what life throws at you just stay strong and keep going.

Patrick Nipp

ABOUT THE AUTHOR

Patrick Nipp is a 16 year old High School junior. He has been writing poetry for about three years. He lives with his parents.

Made in the USA
Coppell, TX
08 April 2022

76224837R00020